D0921231

Literary Sexts
Volume 1

a collection of short & sexy love poems

Edited by
Amanda Oaks & Caitlyn Siehl

WORDS DANCE PUBLISHING
WordsDance.com

Copyright © Words Dance Publishing 2014

No part of this book may be used or performed without written consent from the author except for in critical articles & reviews.

1st Edition
ISBN: 978-0615959726

Cover & Interior Design by Amanda Oaks

Words Dance Publishing
WordsDance.com

Literary Sexts

Volume
1

THIS IS FOR THE LOVERS,
THE POETS,
& THE ONES
WHO KNOW WHAT TO DO
WITH THEIR HANDS

Before I knew you I read myself into all of your love poems.

- TAMMY BREWER

Your name, a game I play, doesn't echo as much as it beats, some deep bass line emerges from the background and hooks me into humming.

- ROBERT LEE BREWER

Mark me like a passage from your favorite book, then open me there again and again.

- TAMMY BREWER

I'm at the park standing next to our pond and watching geese fight over breadcrumbs from children. I'll wait as long as you need me to.

- ROBERT LEE BREWER

You are here, and I dream of tangled trees. I feel your heartbeat in my chest, and taste my perfume dripping from your lips.

- PENELOPE CONNOR

My skin is full of flowerbeds and you know every way to make them bloom.

- ASHE VERNON

My hands will explore new worlds like question marks blazing trails of tautology in close proximity and kindling your limbs into parts of speech.

- JESSICA LAWSON

I am tracing the knobs of your spine like the map of my favorite continent. You are all the places I haven't visited yet and I mark each one off with my teeth.

- ASHE VERNON

Meet me where the now outruns the dogged pursuit of booze-drenched sheets. Meet me where our buried skeletons don't rap on the floorboards.

- DAVID WALKER

Your hands unzip me one breath at a time; there is not room beneath my skin for all of you and I spill over the edges with a sigh.

- ASHE VERNON

You take apart my heart in pieces with your mouth, but the splash of your tongue against mine feeds it back to me. It tastes sweeter coming from you.

- TANYA ROSE

You opened your mouth and spoke the language in my blood.

- ASHE VERNON

You kiss me and there aren't sparks. There's an entire orchestra in my chest, playing staccato on my heart strings.

- TANYA ROSE

You are the slow silt muscle of the pond floor; I am the lost lure sunk there.

- EMILY JEFFRIES

My hands are nomads, my dear desert. May they never find rest.

- LEX BOBROW

Being small things, we understand this as our humble attempt at thunder, at setting the world to shake.

- EMILY JEFFRIES

The pulse of your hips against mine blossoms a bouquet of jasmine flowers behind my eyes.

- LEX BOBROW

Your fingers skate across my frozen pond and melt the snow banks near the edge of the woods.

- KIM KING

You took small, cursive breaths, rose slow like the ocean, swelling to open itself over the shore, relented then fell as if upon some need to return into the sea pulling you back where we began.

- M. K. SUKACH

Delicate work. Like peeling kiwis. My tongue across your skin. Mellow flesh against my lips. Your taste always in my mouth.

- AMY MACLENNAN

How a storms needs to feel the earth how the earth wakes to the pelt of rain how the ground is quenched is how I need you... when my lips are dry for want of what rages in a kiss.

- M. K. SUKACH

My hands were glaciers I never dared to move freely, my fingers icicles. Your touch thawed me to excavation. I want to dig into your warmth.

- GUADALUPE TERRONES

Kiss me like white bread, stick to my teeth even after the whiskey. I want memories of your mouth lodged beneath my tongue to wake me at two in the morning, hungry.

- PATRICK KINDIG

The glass panes of my eyes fog up with our heavy breathing. You write your name into my skin, sweating from the steam our pressed bodies generate.

- GUADALUPE TERRONES

11

When you stretch, I can see the white smile of your hip bone curving above your belt. May your muscles be forever sore.

- PATRICK KINDIG

I want you next to me, in my bed, your clothes making friends with my floor. Love me hard enough so we wake up the neighbors.

- NISHAT AHMED

Your hands peeling that onion, thumbs and forefingers pulling skin from skin—they are sacred. Let me kiss them. Let them bless my sinning chest, let them peel my lips apart.

- PATRICK KINDIG

I don't want to be your harmonies anymore; I want to be the melody you scream when your heart is starving for love. I want to satisfy your hunger.

- NISHAT AHMED

I meet you midway, open-mouthed. My need exhales as the yawning gape of a furnace, as a mouthful of molten air.

- MARYLYN TAN

Show me the parts of you that nobody else ever wanted to sleep with. Show me it all with the lights on.

- NISHAT AHMED

12

We are sails at full tilt in a rudderless ship - you, storming, curve up to meet me. In pelting salt I swallow and blink.

- MARYLYN TAN

You, darling, are Vesuvius. I won't see you coming. Erupt. Wreck me. Leave me ashes, leave me Pompeii, leave me outlined into your history forever.

- NISHAT AHMED

You are dragon-singed artillery at midnight. You come like free-falling bombs, like blooming orchards full of low-hanging fruit.

- MARYLYN TAN

We are sprawled out on your bedroom floor and pretending we are the world. My fingers are the northern wind running through the branches of your hair leaving droplets of stardust and dew everywhere they go.

- NISHAT AHMED

It's not so much that I want to kiss you. I want to relearn vocabulary words from the shape of your mouth. All my poems are yours first.

- YENA SHARMA PURMASIR

Kiss me blossoms in the summer, lover. I want to taste the succulent sweet of your peach tree smile. This time let Adam take the fruit from the garden.

- NISHAT AHMED

13

You taste like cigarettes and blue jolly ranchers and underneath that, the stars that died to make you.

- FORTESA LATIFI

If I could, I'd press my fingers through this screen; hold my favorite parts of you. Force lips through glass to steal a kiss.

- EMBER JANE VAIL

Your moan in my ear: I'd never heard the sound of puddles before. Now they drip music from my lips, and other parts of me. Everywhere, puddles, quivering quietly.

- RACHAEL MADDOX

Surge into me as a downpour, as the pounding waterfall which makes swollen rivers flood, as the sea.

- EMBER JANE VAIL

Your bare belly against mine makes me wanna hibernate 'til the sun shines again in Oregon.

- RACHAEL MADDOX

The happy ending to this night: you tug my hair and lightly brush your hand across my lap. Don't forget how resilient I am and how I would bend for you.

- K WEBER

You fit your mouth over mine like a natural disaster. And I've always loved monsoon season.

- MEGGIE ROYER

You give my hips a soft squeeze as we kiss. We sway and then fall into an embrace that requires our entire selves. Even my lungs are in love as we breathe together.

- K WEBER

I don't just want to take your breath away. I want to rip it from your mouth and keep it locked away between my teeth. You can only have it back if you kiss me again.

- MEGGIE ROYER

Your voice rumbles like thunder in your ribcage; you are the storm to wash away my worries. I always loved walking in the rain.

- CAITLIN HINSHAW

Shuddering - palms leap to claim grounding. But the rush of tongue and skin and sweat keep toes too curled to grip.

- KEENAN JOLLIFF

Last night I dreamt we magnetized our bones. How else could I explain the way we hold each other with a fierceness only atoms dream of?

- CAITLIN HINSHAW

My spine begins anew in its desire to be around you. Weaving, that bones might show tenderness. Tendons lightly playing with the soft flux of your skin.

— KEENAN JOLLIFF

The gentle friction of your hand on my thigh is enough to strike a match inside me. I lean into your lips and the fire blooms and spreads.

— CAITLIN HINSHAW

You exhale. As the tips of my lips mow the plains of your stomach, stopping only momentarily to listen to the secrets of your core.

— KEENAN JOLLIFF

You are an undiscovered continent. I trail my fingers down your mountainsides. Ten explorers digging for buried treasure, I want to take it all.

— ANITA OFOKANSI

Clinging to the cusp of your unveiling I find stillness. And together we unravel into violence.

— KEENAN JOLLIFF

My body is a gospel and you are my first quivering hallelujah. Your breath leaves your mouth like a prayer and washes over me like faith.

— ANITA OFOKANSI

And just like that everything ceased and began anew in the light of me, poised so sweetly against the whole of you.

- KEENAN JOLLIFF

My hands are hungry for your flesh, desperate in the way that rivers empty themselves over waterfalls, committing suicide on the rocks below.

- ANITA OFOKANSI

My ear clings to your back, a barnacle eavesdropping on your whispering stomach. It drips—sea salt, jasmine tea—it's the most beautiful sound in the world. It sings you're here.

- J. AUGUST

Our bodies becomes battlefields and we make love like this is war. Drop kisses like grenades until all that's left is silence and smoke clearing.

- ANITA OFOKANSI

My lips are the breeze pouring in through the open window, brushing off dust to lick the light floating through your chapel carved in the mountain mouth.

- J. AUGUST

I peel back your skin to see if we have the same scars. I follow the map of your veins back to your heart and press my palm against yours to tangle our lifelines.

- ANITA OFOKANSI

I hope to breathe in you. I hope my body will be the blood your roots drink.

- J. AUGUST

I swallow the sun and light up like a burning house with flames for eyes and a smoking mouth. You pick up my ashes and tuck them into your back pocket.

- ANITA OFOKANSI

The line where your eyelids press gently together: the horizon on a landscape where the sky is your breath and the earth is tonight, sleeping here.

- J. AUGUST

I slip rocks into your pockets to weigh you down. My heart is a river trying to run in every direction. You sing me a song underwater and drown with a smile.

- ANITA OFOKANSI

Your neck is inked like the squeeze depths of a sea my tongue dreams of sailing, my tongue tying knots into the back of my teeth, practicing, waiting for a night with a salty breeze and the moon's dark waves.

- J. AUGUST

We commit sins in holy places, fold ourselves between pews like dirty pictures tucked into a bible. Pant each other's names until they sound like scripture.

- ANITA OFOKANSI

When you dance, you stamp your seal into the clay earth as if to say, *this is the spot where I exist*, meaning, *this is the spot where I love*, as if the entirety of my being wasn't acutely aware of that already.

- J. AUGUST

You rediscover me like the rotting skeleton of a sunken ship and pull me out of the sea. I thank you for saving me and you tell me I am not a tragedy.

- ANITA OFOKANSI

My tongue collides with your collarbone like a meteor careening across the cosmos, and I taste the stars you are made of.

- TRICIA SMITH

You kiss me with your mouth wide open like you're not afraid of swallowing poison. I taste the good and bad in you and want them both. We call this bravery.

- ANITA OFOKANSI

My hand is tangled in your hair as though trapped in the tendrils of a comet traveling through space. I can sense the entire universe through your scalp.

- TRICIA SMITH

All the shadow selves you and I clutch in the dark, dance in the open doorway of loving—bruises and safe words inside the smack of tango.

- DAVE MALONE

19

You, benevolent god, legs splayed like instruments of creation. I, blank slate of the universe, kneel in wait for you to fill me with your hot, honeyed light.

- AMBER DECKER

Our backs break in loving—and then the rest of us. Your cave nose, my lily ankle.

- DAVE MALONE

You send long tongues of fire sweeping like rivers under my skin. The fish have learned to speak your name in many languages. In whispers, they beg you to come and drink.

- AMBER DECKER

You glow glimmer fire supernova through the night ruining sky, shutting down cities— this end of the world star fire you are quiets the world.

- DAVE MALONE

My hands are suntanned tourists without a map whose desire compels them onward to explore your golden cities by the light of the stars.

- AMBER DECKER

The moment between your thighs where I become a devout follower of your existence. That hour which passes in slow seconds of soft skin, as I lay my head against you, drifting, drowsy with love.

- BRITTAN LULFS

Your lips settle at the curve of my navel, a blanket of whispers falling on my skin like soft yellow leaves.

- AMBER DECKER

With eyes wide and hands hungry I am reaching for you and digging into your skin to find your center and bathe in it.

- BRITTAN LULFS

Your grin is a flash of primal fire in the dark. Somewhere deep inside me, something hungry wakens and shifts, uncurls its insatiable tongue.

- AMBER DECKER

I have been thinking of how I want to be touched by you, with hands that will play me like piano keys, with fingers that will make a symphony out of me.

- KARESE BURROWS

You till the soil of my need, my lips a blood-red flower bursting open with the first wet flush of your heat.

- AMBER DECKER

Your lips cover me like rain and every night I am turned into a hurricane.

- KARESE BURROWS

Your name is a tsunami, some exquisite violence flooding my lungs and bubbling up from my mouth without warning.

- S.T. GIBSON

When it comes right down to it, all that nonsense about hearts syncing up feels like a hallelujah with our bodies pressed together like praying hands.

- D.M. ALEXANDER

I am war drum, with goose pimpled skin pulled tight over a hollow chest and a heart that strikes up a battle rhythm every time you touch me.

- S.T. GIBSON

Daydreaming of running my fingers down your spine as if you were my favorite book. I want torn pages and I want smudged words.

- DARCY VINES

Every time, you peel back my skin, pry open my ribs, and feast on my insides. Every time, you make a meal of my heart, and every time, I let you.

- S.T. GIBSON

You're not one for poetry or sentimentality, so I'll just say that I've dreamt of being the motor oil trapped in the grooves of your weathered hands.

- DARCY VINES

22

I ache for your hum between my legs, the purring of motorcycles on winding highways: wind in my hair, and romance in losing myself to the sweet, revving vibration of the engine again and again.

- NICOLE SWANSON

You smile and it's like sunrise. Something inside me Wakes up, stretching.

- B. PAVLIK

Our mouths are beginning to taste the same because they don't remember they are separate.

- NICOLE SWANSON

The miracle of your hair as it spills over my chest: the soft curls sewing my broken heart back together.

- HEATHER ROSE DONKERS

Honey drips too slow, and I can almost feel the buzzing. Your lips are a beehive, just out of reach.

- CALEB HAMILTON

I float away in cool sheets against my burning skin, and you are the sea guiding me beyond the realm of earthly things.

- ROSE IRIE

My lipstick spills over your mouth and trickles down to your chin, your neck, pooling into your collarbones. We love like crushed grapes in wine country.

— CAITLYN SIEHL

I'm standing at the edge of the woods, arms stretched out parallel with the tree line, head snapped back like a branch. My skin awakens like leaves from a dream on the ground. You are the wind. I can hear you coming.

— AMANDA OAKS

You're kissing a wildfire up my thigh and I am tracing the landscape of your jawbone like a sculptor. My hands were made for this.

— CAITLYN SIEHL

I balloon, a raindrop with its arms wrapped around a tree limb. It's always been pinpricks or too much weight that caused the bust. But you, you shook the whole damn tree causing all of me to fall & soak into the ground.

— AMANDA OAKS

You are laying beside me and my hand is splayed like a starfish across your chest. I can feel the ocean in my fingertips.

— CAITLYN SIEHL

The rush you give me: The way a blade of grass must feel when splashed with a cloud's cry after days of screaming for rain.

— AMANDA OAKS

The sky is blushing the color of your chest. The clouds look like your collarbones.

- CAITLYN SIEHL

Clouds drape overhead, little pockets of flare-up. I seek you out from under a whisper. This bare silence, before the spread of Spring.

- AMANDA OAKS

I'm kissing your mouth and it feels like telling the truth. I'm kissing your neck and a volcano is waking up after 100 years of silence.

- CAITLYN SIEHL

You push me to that strange somewhere between human & animal, back & forth I go, a paper boat soon to sink like sheet-burn on the tops of both feet.

- AMANDA OAKS

We are the fall of Rome, all fire and fighting. We collapse into each other like the pieces of the Parthenon, kissing like gladiators, loving like rebuilding.

- CAITLYN SIEHL

You creep into my head like a river rushing for the sea & a cosmic digit of fingertips flash over me.

- AMANDA OAKS

You are pressing against me like I press flowers against the pages in my book. You are kissing my neck and it feels like the start of forever. I want to touch you until my palms burn.

— AMIRAE GARCIA

The wet of your mouth rains down my neck like frame, the soft heat of your tongue burns the apple in my throat. We are practiced at this love that asks angels to cover their eyes and turns devils shy.

— ZACHARY KLUCKMAN

I think your eyes are filled with hurricanes and I'll stand in front of them, willing your waters to touch every part of me.

— AMIRAE GARCIA

I melt into the gentleness of your fingertips. Your tongue presses me open like the summer fresh flesh of a perfectly ripe fig, all juice, seeds and pulp.

— KRISTIN PROCTER

The small of your back is refuge, is veldt, is summer heat. And I am predatory snarl.

— STEVE BRIGHTMAN

The steam builds just beneath a whistle, you calculate precisely. You seize the kettle. Pour. Stroke the tea bag in and out, then top it off with cream.

— KRISTIN PROCTER

26

I can't brush out the taste of you; coffee breath, cigarette smoke, and all. Mouth to mouth; Our shared vices linger on each other. Your salt still lives in my tongue.

- BRANDON SPECK

Construction has forced me to drive slowly over coarsely grated concrete, like the rough red ridges of your tongue this morning.

- KRISTIN PROCTER

f; your violin body, closed eyes, pressed fingers, we moan beautiful harmonies.

- BRANDON SPECK

Ocean floods in, takes me tumbling & breaks me open on the rocks. Tide rolls out slowly, leaves me beached, salty. You comb my hair back, fingernails drag across my scalp.

- LARA BLACKADAAR

I'll take you quiet as the bones in your closet, love as softly as a whisper. Holding your tongue like a secret.

- RUSSELL SILVA

I dreamt last night of your teeth on my skin. Blood rose from the sea of wounds like the coils of an exultant leviathan. I am drowning.

- MICHAEL CANTIN

You smiled and lit up like the dusk. I sank to your lips like the sun against the horizon. We made the day stand still.

- RUSSELL SILVA

I want to kiss you until you melt into me, ice turning to water. I want to drink you deep, and warm you from the inside.

- NICOLA CAYLESS

Every dress you wear is a loaded gun, and we play a game of Russian Roulette with every kiss. And tonight: Tonight I am playing to lose.

- MICHAEL CANTIN

Poetry is the way I fuck you when you're gone.

- NICOLA CAYLESS

TO BE CONTINUED IN 2015...

volume 2

Bios

NISHAT AHMED: I'm currently a sophomore at the University of Illinois Urbana-Champaign studying Psychology and Poetry. I have an avid love for pop punk and cheesy romance novels. If you want to know more about me, listen to Fall Out Boy, Andrea Gibson and/or read a John Green novel.

D.M. ALEXANDER: I've loved lots, loved and lost, loved lost lovers, and if I regretted anything, it would have to be that I've always avoided saying the words. So - here's to saying them, in a million different pieces, places, and ways. Thank you so very much for reading.

J. AUGUST: I'm currently an undergraduate at the University of Southern California. I think of all the results of words on an audience, no effect is quite as satisfying as a swoon. Being able to make someone stop and sigh, that's a unique relationship between author and reader--it's a communion of the most vital energy found in the universe: love.

LARA BLACKADAAR: When my Canadian hands aren't frozen to the keyboard, I enjoy reading, playing with my dogs, and making naughty-looking pastry. The only subject I'm prudish about is proper grammar.

LEX BOBROW: All you really need to know about me is that more than anything--at my core--I want to be captivating and therefore powerful.

ROBERT LEE BREWER: My first non-assignment poem was written to woo a girl in high school. That's how it began. I use "literary sexting" on my wife to this day, and she, thankfully, continues to retaliate.

TAMMY FOSTER BREWER: Author of the chapbook, *No Glass Allowed* (Words Dance Publishing) - I typed I love you to my (now) husband over gmail chat before I ever even heard his voice. I can be reached at tammyfbrewer@gmail.com.

STEVE BRIGHTMAN: I live in Ohio and spend most of my summers facing the ballyard. All my other seasons I spend facing her.

KARESE BURROWS: I am a twenty year old college student from The Bahamas. With one more semester to go, I'm gearing up to graduate with an Associates in Art. I have high hopes to go on to study creative writing, photography and art history. I have been writing poetry ever since I was thirteen years old. When I'm not writing, you can find me curled up some-where with my nose in a book.

MICHAEL CANTIN: I wish nothing more than to gift you a smile or the slight rise of an eyebrow, dear reader. These words, short and concise, are to be the genesis of something unknown, something shared, something greater.

NICOLA CAYLESS: I'm a poet who takes her espressos without sugar, and reads Neruda on public transport. More of my work can be found at: http://moderateclimates.com.

PENELOPE CONNOR: I'm an ink-stained, messy, polyamorous poet-girl who feels years younger than my four-decades-and-change. Like the grinch, my heart grew three sizes one day! So, I fill my life with two long-term loves, two-hundred-fifty miles apart. I'm blessed with a bevy of friends, am addicted to vocabulary, and have embarrassing penmanship.

AMBER DECKER: I am a Scorpio with an Aries moon, so I reasoned that poetry was my only chance at holding on to my sanity. I am in love with love, and I will always believe in the undeniable power of really awesome, world-shattering sex. And full-moons. Those are nice, too.

HEATHER ROSE DONKERS: I'm a believer in purposeful todays and hopeful tomorrows. Just like each of us, I will one day change the world with my words and passions. I promise to choose them wisely. This one is for you.

AMIRAE GARCIA: I'm a twenty year-old pogonophile that lives in a small town in California. I like hot tea, quotes, and you. :)

S.T. GIBSON: I'm a plucky undergrad who enjoys theology, musical theater, tea, and leaving my loved ones affectionate little scraps of poetry in embarrassing public places.

CALEB HAMILTON: I am an eccentric little speck from Oklahoma with dreams the size of planets. I like candy, puzzles, snow, tobacco, and every kind of art. My words are an effort to paint the sounds my heart makes. I hope you can understand them.

CAITLIN HINSHAW: Your average directionless dweller of the physical realm. I find beauty in science. Looking for a cure for death and heartbreak, but will settle for immortalization through words. Or ice cream.

ROSE IRIE: A seeker of magic in everyday things. A flame desperate to set things on fire. A brimming cup of words and a white blank page. A heart expressed in cursive words on good days and spilled ink on bad ones. Love is my muse, my muse is my love, and he doesn't even know.

EMILY JEFFRIES: I live and work in Toronto where I am currently completing my MA in Creative Writing at the University of Toronto.

KEENAN JOLLIFF: I am an actor, a dancer, and a poet. Originally from Boulder, Colorado, I now live in NYC. I write with my wonderful friend Nick Smerkanich. Together we have a collaboration called Blood & Inc. Our first published work is a self titled collection of pieces from the past 2 years. www.blood&inc.com

PATRICK KINDIG: I'm from Lansing, Michigan, and currently a graduate student at Indiana University. I do not sext in real life, as my first and only attempt at it as an undergrad ended disastrously. My poetry has been published or is forthcoming in Poiesis Review, Isthmus, Prick of the Spindle, and the Jabberwock Review.

KIM KING: Bonjour! I was raised in Western New York, but I lived and studied in France which opened my eyes and ears to the sexiest language and food on the planet. My poems have been published in various journals and anthologies while I complete my MA in Writing at The Johns Hopkins University. Vive l'amour!

ZACHARY KLUCKMAN: I have been writing since I realized DaVinci had already done what I wanted with a canvas. I've represented Albuquerque twice at the National Poetry Slam and have 2 full length collections of work out, "Animals in our Flesh" and "Some of it is Muscle". String cheese confuses me.

FORTESA LATIFI: I'm a 20-year old senior at the University of Arizona. After graduation, I plan to move to New York and become a total cliche. My parents named me after a book and my love of words remains to this day the only thing I am entirely sure of. I breathe in poems like they'll save me- and they have so far.

JESSICA LAWSON: I'm a 26-year-old office manager of a medical practice. I've always had a passion for collecting words that make me feel alive and inspired. I spend my free time drawing, painting, writing, and creating.

BRITTAN LULFS: Twenty-three years young, and all I am is love; though only shown to me in fragmented rays of sunlight, I was born with a heart three sizes too big. I am an old soul in a new world, navigating life through love and writing. I hope you find solace in me.

AMY MACLENNAN: I've been published in Hayden's Ferry Review, River Styx, Linebreak, Cimarron Review, Painted Bride Quarterly, Folio, and Rattle. My chapbook, The Fragile Day, was released from Spire Press in the summer of 2011, and my chapbook, Weathering, was published by Uttered Chaos Press in early 2012.

RACHAEL MADDOX: Volcanic and snake-like, I like eruptions and seductions. I'm messing around with both in Portland, OR where ecstatic dance and hula hooping in my candle-lit bedroom keep me alive. You can find me online at rachaelmaddox.com. But the truth is, I prefer in-person happenstance and magical encounters.

DAVE MALONE: I like short poems, and I love this anthology's premise. I hail from the Ozarks where brevity is appreciated. In 2012, one of my Twitter poems aired on the "Muses and Metaphor" series from NPR's Tell Me More. I publish a bi-monthly e-newsletter, If I Had a Nickel, whose title derives from the sentiment of my rascally grandfather.

AMANDA OAKS: I found a red & tattered spiral notebook when I was 12. It was my mom's, she copied poems in it when she was in high school, poems that she found & loved. I read through it a handful of times & in turn started to experiment with language. I wrote of heartbreak. Heartbreak at a 7th grade level & in ABCB format but heartbreak nonetheless. I printed them out on our dot matrix printer & I passed them out to all my girlfriends. That's when my love affair with writing & "publishing" poetry began.

ANITA OFOKANSI: Long story short, I'm a hurricane without a name. A force of nature, more storm than girl. Take shelter. I'll protect you if I can, but baby I'll wreck you if I get the chance. Love me if you dare. You can be my beautiful disaster.

B. PAVLIK: I'm a college freshman. I've been writing poetry and prose for about seven years.

KRISTIN PROCTER: I am a motherwriter who lives in Massachusetts, was born in Canada, married a Brit and birthed two Australian babies. I like knitting, yoga and conversations best avoided in polite company. Luckily I have never been mistaken for polite company. I wrote my birth story for First Time Mum.

YENA SHARMA PURMASIR: I'm a 21 year old poet, skilled in quick text replies and the art of curving a sentence into a subtle winky-face. I have been licking my own lips for years. When my first book of poetry was released, I was wearing swimming bottoms as underwear.

TANYA ROSE: I am no longer Little Girl Lost but Little Girl Finding, 19 years old and hailing from an eternally rainy city. Half hot-blooded Italian, half infuriatingly polite Canadian. I am fueled by words, music, travel and confrontation. I post my words at heardthecoldwindsay.tumblr.com

MEGGIE ROYER: I'm a writer and photographer in love with love poems. I've been published in Words Dance Magazine, Winter Tangerine Review, Fameless Magazine, and more, and won medals in the 2013 National Scholastic Art & Writing Awards. Poetry is my life and the blood in my veins.

CAITLYN SIEHL: I'm a junior in college and currently studying journalism and film, mastering the art of being human. I write poetry in my tiny apartment and hope to, someday, infuse my love for words and my love for film together in order to become a screenwriter.

RUSSELL SILVA: I go by my stage name "AttentionAllRomantics", I'm a local poet and songwriter of West Covina, California. As well as a spoken word and prose poet, I enjoy playing the guitar, piano, ukulele, and sing to make my reflections on love heard.

TRICIA SMITH: Amazing, dipped in awesome, covered in bitch sprinkles. Bibliophile. Melomaniac. HTML/CSS/JS wrangler. Mother. Lover. Friend. Sapiosexual. Dreamer. Basorexic. INFJ

BRANDON SPECK: I'm a semi-professional dishwasher that is still trying to figure out this whole living business while living in Portland, Oregon. When I'm not scrubbing pint glasses, I'm designing books and covers for Where Are You Press.

M.K. SUKACH: My fiction and poetry appears or is forthcoming in a number of venues to include The Sow's Ear Poetry Review, The Hamilton Stone Review, Ontologica, theNewerYork, Cellpoems, Poetry Northeast, The Blast Furnace, and The Citron Review. mksukach.com

NICOLE SWANSON: I grew up in Minnesota, believing that the wind moving over the plains carried with it the stories behind so many sighs. My writing is inspired by hoar frost and classical music and the exchange of glances between strangers. : tongue-tiedprose.tumblr.com

GUADALUPE TERRONES: Hello lovelies. I'm 18 and live in wonderfully exhausting New York City. A few of my addictions include Latin, french fries, 500 Days of Summer, and books beyond number. If your kindness does wish to find more of my writing, my tumblr is masochistic-dreamers.

EMBER JANE VAIL: I am a trans woman living in Ottawa Canada with my very lovely partner, who may or may not receive this as a gift at some point. Though I write poetry and the occasional story, my main focus is in writing and performing music.

ASHE VERNON: I have been writing ever since I can remember. Currently I am going to university: majoring in theatre with a minor in gender studies. I'd like to be a playwright and have had two of my original plays produced as staged readings.

DARCY VINES: I'm a 19 year old English major at Aquinas College, learning the rules so I know how to shatter them later, and if my mom finds out I wrote anything even mildly related to a sext she'll implode. Here's to being sexy with words and not skin.

DAVID WALKER: I love to teach, write, and hang out with my fiancée, Caitlin. My fiction and poetry appears or is forthcoming in Words Dance, Cactus Heart, MadHat, Diversion Press, Paper Nautilus, and others. I can always be contacted at dwalker8508@yahoo.com.

K WEBER: I am a software tester, an online DJ and an extremely part-time poet. I live outside of Cincinnati and can often be found in love with one thing or everything or nothing at all. Visit midwesternskirt.com for information on my projects including my 2012 collection of poems, Bluest Grey.

Other titles available from
WORDS DANCE PUBLISHING

LOVE AND OTHER SMALL WARS

Poetry by Donna-Marie Riley

| $12 | 76 pages | 5.5" x 8.5" | softcover |

ISBN: 978-0615931111

Love and Other Small Wars reminds us that when you come back from combat usually the most fatal of wounds are not visible. Riley's debut collection is an arsenal of deeply personal poems that embody an intensity that is truly impressive yet their hands are tender. She enlists you. She gives you camouflage & a pair of boots so you can stay the course through the minefield of her heart. You will track the lovely flow of her soft yet fierce voice through a jungle of powerful imagery on womanhood, relationships, family, grief, sexuality & love, amidst other matters. Battles with the heart aren't easily won but Riley hits every mark. You'll be relieved that you're on the same side. Much like war, you'll come back from this book changed.

"Riley's work is wise, intense, affecting, and uniquely crafted. This collection illuminates her ability to write with both a gentle hand and a bold spirit. She inspires her readers and creates an indelible need inside of them to consume more of her exceptional poetry. I could read *Love and Other Small Wars* all day long...and I did."

— **APRIL MICHELLE BRATTEN**
editor of *Up the Staircase Quarterly*

"Riley's poems are personal, lyrical and so vibrant they practically leap off the page, which also makes them terrifying at times. A beautiful debut."

— **BIANCA STEWART**

Other titles available from
WORDS DANCE PUBLISHING

Unrequited love? We've all been there.

Enter:

WHAT TO DO AFTER SHE SAYS NO
by Kris Ryan.

This skillfully designed 10-part poem explores what it's like to ache for someone. This is the book you buy yourself or a friend when you are going through a breakup or a one-sided crush, it's the perfect balance between aha, humor & heartbreak.

WHAT TO DO AFTER SHE SAYS NO
A Poem by Kris Ryan

$10 | 104 pages | 5" x 8" | softcover | ISBN: 978-0615870045

"*What to Do After She Says No* takes us from Shanghai to the interior of a refrigerator, but mostly dwells inside the injured human heart, exploring the aftermath of emotional betrayal. This poem is a compact blast of brutality, with such instructions as "Climb onto the roof and jump off. If you break your leg, you are awake. If you land without injury, pinch and twist at your arm until you wake up." Ryan's use of the imperative often leads us to a reality where pain is the only outcome, but this piece is not without tenderness, and certainly not without play, with sounds and images ricocheting off each other throughout. Anticipate the poetry you wish you knew about during your last bad breakup; this poem offers a first "foothold to climb out" from that universal experience."

— LISA MANGINI

"Reading Kris Ryan's *What To Do After She Says No* is like watching your heart pound outside of your chest. Both an unsettling visual experience and a hurricane of sadness and rebirth—this book demands more than just your attention, it takes a little bit of your soul, and in the end, makes everything feel whole again."

— JOHN DORSEY
author of ***Tombstone Factory***

"*What to Do After She Says No* is exquisite. Truly, perfectly exquisite. It pulls you in on a familiar and wild ride of a heart blown open and a mind twisting in an effort to figure it all out. It's raw and vibrant...and in the same breath comforting. I want to crawl inside this book and live in a world where heartache is expressed so magnificently.

— JO ANNA ROTHMAN
MA, Coach & Conjurer of Electric Creative Wholeness

WORDS DANCE PUBLISHING has one aim:

To spread mind-blowing / heart-opening poetry.

Words Dance artfully & carefully wrangles words that were born to dance wildly in the heart-mind matrix. Rich, edgy, raw, emotionally-charged energy balled up & waiting to whip your eyes wild; we rally together words that were written to make your heart go boom right before they slay your mind. You dig?

Words Dance Publishing is an independent press out of Pennsylvania. We work closely & collaboratively with all of our writers to ensure that their words continue to breathe in a sound & stunning home. Most importantly though, we leave the windows in these homes unlocked so you, the reader, can crawl in & throw one fuck of a house party.

To learn more about our books, authors, events & Words Dance Poetry Magazine, visit:

WORDSDANCE.COM